Tile

poems by

Gregory Luce

Finishing Line Press
Georgetown, Kentucky

Title

Copyright © 2016 by Gregory Luce
ISBN 978-1-944251-79-6 First Edition
All rights reserved under International and Pan-American Copyright Conventions. No part of this book may be reproduced in any manner whatsoever without written permission from the publisher, except in the case of brief quotations embodied in critical articles and reviews.

ACKNOWLEDGMENTS

Some of these poems have been previously published—sometimes in slightly different form—as follows:

"Assorted Landscapes," "Standing Out in the Rain," *The Rusty Nail*
"And we ran," *VQR Instagram*
"Finzel Swamp," "After Snow," *Northern Virginia Review*
"Tile," *The Hydeout*
"February Wind," "Ascent," "End of November," *Broadkill Review*
"An Ordinary Evening," *Cactus Heart*
"Over Coffee," Commonthought
"Mixing Memory and Desire," *Almost 5/Q*
"Transfigured," *Rising Tide Review*

Editor: Christen Kincaid

Cover Art: Gregory Luce

Author Photo: Brian Gordon Green

Cover Design: Elizabeth Maines

Printed in the USA on acid-free paper.
Order online: www.finishinglinepress.com
also available on amazon.com

Author inquiries and mail orders:
Finishing Line Press
P. O. Box 1626
Georgetown, Kentucky 40324
U. S. A.

Table of Contents

Assorted Landscapes 1

And we ran 2

Finzel Swamp 3

The Mechanism of Joy 4

Tile 8

Dream of Hands 9

Standing Out in the Rain 10

February Wind 11

Mind of Winter 12

After Snow 13

A Taste of Wind 14

An Ordinary Evening 15

Over Coffee 16

Ascent 17

Parallel Lines 19

End of November 20

Mixing Memory and Desire 21

Tranesque 23

Turn Away 24

Lost and Found 25

Sunday Afternoon 26

Transfigured 27

To the memory of my mother, Patricia, and my father, Warren. And as always, for Naomi, most lovely tile in the mosaic of my life.

Assorted Landscapes

The desert is easy to love
but hard to live with.
It's a difficult place to get a drink.

The ocean seduces with whispers
and caresses then withdraws
leaving you gasping and wriggling
on a rough wet surface.

Mountains stand imperious and remote
above you. They lure you up
on a hand-to-hand climb
and take your breath
and leave you cold.

Friend, or stranger, move along,
there's nothing for you here.

And we ran

crazily like children
in the first downpour
after long drought
each damp breath
an exaltation
droplets flung like silver
from our hair our feet crashing
splayed into grass then lifting
off the small depressions
filling and blades springing
up again

Finzel Swamp

Fog hangs low
and soggy over
this wet ground.
Who knew fog
had so many shades:
almost colorless just above
the grass, pale gray above
that, charcoal next,
and finally white at the top,
a few slender old bare
trees poking up,
tips of the limbs
barely visible,
the surrounding mountains
shrouded unseen.
Currents course through
the brown pond waters
and two snakes coil
around each other,
seeking warmth
in the soaked grass.
Visibility low
but the songs
of innumerable birds
fill the heavy air.
Feet soaked, shivering,
I pick out
the piercing melody
of a Swamp sparrow
trilling through
the slowly lightening fog.

The Mechanism of Joy

I.
It rumbles into life
an undercurrent
under the sidewalk
or like a distant
trill of piano carried
across the courtyard
on a late-evening breeze,
a thin current of
water flowing under the skin
of ice on the creek, blood
throbbing warm in the veins
on the back of the hand, or
the phone vibrating in
my pocket when I know
who's calling unasked for
and unearned.

II.

Dancing on the edge
of the subway platform,
skating alongside the crack
in the ice, running
on the flat concrete top
of the brick wall,
electric pulses shooting
down my arms and up
the back of my neck,
fine hairs on end,
panic joy of skipping steps
going down, the near-fall
on the icy patch
of sidewalk, exhilaration
of finding my footing
just in time.

III.

Yes, I dance on the edge
of the Metro platform
sometimes, it's 5:07 say,
and I just escaped
the office and a train
is coming to take me
to see my sons,
or uptown to sit
with the sangha,
or—happy day!—
my lover will be waiting
in Virginia, and who
could stand still
with the iPod playing Wilco,
"Take Me Back to Tulsa," Nina
Simone's "Feeling Good," or
L. Cohen: "Dance Me
to the End of Love."

IV.

Ecstasy—*ex-stasis*: displace, stand outside or
I could be hovering
inches above the floorboards
when she floats in
all legs and tresses
clothes billowing as
light pours in
from every direction
and dust motes pulse
like electric particles
percolating up my spine,
breath is slow
and rich and fills
the room and we float
in lazy orbit.

Tile

I laid it out for you
like tiles black and white
on the bathroom floor
and you still wouldn't see
it you kept adding
yellow or red and
it's such a simple pattern
I can replicate
until it hits the wall.

Dream of Hands

Bruce Nauman, 15 Pairs of Hands,
National Gallery of Art, Washington, DC

I.
clasped hands gently
touching fists
open palms turned
outward veined
backs rippling knuckles
bulging into ridges
delicate drape of hand
over fist frame
of thumb touching
finger touching thumb

II.
the body as a whole
on the whole often ungainly
parts moving independently
right not knowing what
left is doing head
ruling and controlling
nothing but what if
hands could dance
alone or paired
clasp each other
make fists and strike
grip pen or brush touch
keys strings manipulate
themselves

III.
do hands dream
of freedom
from grasping?

Standing Out in the Rain

I looked up at the saturated sky
and tried to see it
as a layer of silver air
spread level and smooth
just above my head but
a few fat drops fell on me,
then a crow tore a hole in it
getting away quick,
the lightning started,
rain percolated
through my shirt.
I shivered and turned
to walk indoors
and suddenly
I was in the air
alongside the crow,
arcing up then leveling off
above the clouds, winging
toward the sun
dead ahead, its light
streaming out like the tails
of an enormous kite,
and beyond it deep blue dusk.
I shook myself all over
and I was standing
in the doorway, looking up
at two ragged holes
in the dripping sky.

February Wind

Yes it does howl
even here this far
from the Plains
and my windows held
though my door rattled
until I shoved
a matchbook into the frame.

I finally slept
but some wind was still
moaning inside my head
and I woke up shivering
but not cold.

And I'm still thinking
about it days later:
That wind brought
something back.

I am moving around
the rim of memory
looking in
and the wind,
the wind without end
blows across the tops
of the tall grass
and makes waves in
this endless inland sea.

Mind of Winter

Regard the purity
of fresh snowfall
under the icy moon
before sunlight washes
over and it crusts
and darkens to the color
of ash or soot.
The cold dry wind
sweeps over it
and whispers
forget forget forget
to hold nothing
in the mind
is everything.

After Snow

The sheet of snow is
drawing back at the edges.
On a branch
a black rag—no,
it shakes itself
into form—a crow
perched observant.
The crow's obsidian eye
ranges over the field
noting slowly emerging
prizes: a bit of fat
clinging to a bone,
a scatter of cigarette
butts, a cheese-smeared
wrapper, a crumpled cup.

The crow drops
and picks and sorts,
its splayed feet
imprinting stars
in the crust of snow.

A Taste of Wind

A man walks up the street
into the wind. He can't
decide if the warmth under
the chill is a promise
or a final breath, seasons
balancing on a knife's edge,
but a dull one, a table knife
perhaps, gleaming dully.
If placed on the tongue
it would leave the metallic taste
he tastes in his mouth right now.
As he nears his door he almost
walks past, bracing into the wind,
but he thinks of a chair and a pen,
and the cold water that might
dispel the taste in his mouth
so he turns and goes in.

An Ordinary Evening

I've washed my hands
about six times tonight
and brushed my teeth,
not rituals, just ordinary
ablutions on an ordinary night.
Now time to read before
sleep: a little poetry,
Henry James on the novel.
When I turn the light off
the heater will hum
like the car engine,
me lying in the back seat
watching lights smear
the windows, a few stars,
barely hearing the buzz
of voices on the radio.

Over Coffee

Nothing happens *because*
he says everything
is contingent like
the steam from his cup
rising in random
intricate patterns
between them as
they talked over coffee
almost forgetting to drink
their eyes meeting
through the steam
then she lowers
hers and regards
the surface of the
coffee in her cup
following the rise
of the steam upward
look at the steam
she says.

Ascent

Appalling neglect
he thinks resting
on one knee
retying his shoe
on the cracked tiles
of the station platform
by summer there
will be weeds growing
here and he stands
too quickly so that
his eyes go a little spotty
and his head spins
until he takes one
deep breath and starts
a stride to the escalator
broken again damn it
and sways a little
climbing to the street
a bit short of breath
from the too high steps
as he pulls himself
together ash lands
on his sleeve from
a young woman's
passing cigarette
he flicks it away irritated
when a light trill catches
his ear and he looks up
just in time to glimpse
a House finch before

it's startled into flight
so he goes grinning
along the sidewalk
barely noticing the accretion
of cigarette butts underfoot
and hardly disgusted at all.

Parallel Lines

I have made you complicit,
a character in my formerly
one-man show:
Had the train been more
crowded or you more bored
it could have been a speaking part,
but you had space around you
and something pleasant on your mind.
It wasn't your flowered blouse
or your high heels or even
your luxuriant hair, no,
it was that distracted smile
that made me look across
the aisle a second time
and a third but your eyes
continued gazing upward.
Still, you got off at my stop.
I looked back once
as I was going through the gate
to see you smiling
in my direction and we
ended up ascending
on parallel escalators,
then you went east,
I went west,
and there was no Act II.

End of November

> *"I found myself more truly and more strange."*
> —Wallace Stevens

After work crossword finished,
taste of coffee still lingering,
I flip through the paper.
Brad Pitt is having
an existential crisis
(though his hair is perfect).
I toss the paper
in the bin and step outside.
Even after dark it's not
too cold for the last day
of November and I don't
feel like going home
this early on Friday night
so I make my way
down Irving Street breaching
the flow of legs and bodies
in each direction, lights dazzling
as I consider where
to have dinner, round
the corner onto 14th
and unexpectedly there
I am looking back at me
from a shop window,
headlights sliding along
the glass. I stop and regard
myself perhaps as passing
strangers see me, wide-eyed
and white-haired, then turn
away into a light gust
of wind and a sudden
slight chill.

Mixing Memory and Desire

It *was* in April, yes,
I was on a plane
somewhere over Alabama
halfway home
from Texas, sunset
receding behind
as we flew on
into the night,
suspended between Earth
and the stars, my son
dozing a few seats away,
and you know that feeling
you get when flying,
especially at night, the way
you hardly seem to be
moving and time itself
has almost stopped,
what I'm getting at
here is that sense
of hanging, Dallas
somewhere behind,
Washington far ahead
in the dark,
my mother laid away
barely two days before,
ashes carefully placed
into the small crypt,
winter over in Texas,
a warm and lovely Saturday,
sun flooding the church
garden already in flower,

and I was wondering
if it was still cold in
Washington, but
when we finally landed
it was raining and warm.

Good Friday came
with rain again,
two weeks gone by
and no one else died.

Tranesque

The very thought of you
after one long evening
of talk cascades
through my mind
like music, like
your hair over
your shoulders
in the flickering
candlelight as the breeze
grew chill and your voice
came warm across
the small space between
us, your words,
too, cascading like
notes, like Trane
soloing filigrees.

Turn Away

Desire doesn't
die it sinks into
the blood like
water into an
underground stream
and then often rises
just under skin's
surface. For example
I have seen a man . . .
but to speak truly
when the sight of
your face
pricks my heart
like a tiny needle
I start to reach
or call out but
instead I turn
away and take
one deep breath
my skin tingling as
blood pulses hot
just underneath.

Lost and Found

I got lost in your eyes
so it was good
when you rested your head
in the crook of my arm
it was warm and
we could breathe together
then you sat up
and faced me
can I kiss you I asked
forgetting my grammar
and you said simply
yes.

Sunday Afternoon

We talk across bare wood
floor unpolished
surface veined
with cracks dust
glitters in the shaft
of light between us
the shadow beneath
the window grows.

Transfigured

I turn off the lamp
lean on the balcony rail
drawing in night air
damp almost palpable
wisps of fog hovering
bats gone only a few
crickets punctuating the silence
after harsh words
the glow from streetlamps
soothes I take one more
deep draught then turn
and go inside.

Gregory Luce is the author of the chapbooks *Signs of Small Grace* (Pudding House Publications) and *Drinking Weather* (Finishing Line Press), and the collection *Memory and Desire* (Sweatshoppe Publications). His poems have appeared in numerous print and online journals, and in the anthologies *Living in Storms* (Eastern Washington University Press) *and Bigger than They Appear* (Accents Publishing). In 2014, he was awarded the Larry Neal Award for adult poetry by the Arts and Humanities Commission of Washington D.C. He lives in Arlington, Virginia.

www.ingramcontent.com/pod-product-compliance
Lightning Source LLC
Chambersburg PA
CBHW060226050426
42446CB00013B/3186